KNOCK KNOCK, UNICORN WHO?

ILLUSTRATED UNICORN & MERMAID JOKES

Stephanie Rodriguez

Jenna Johnston

xist Publishing

Text Copyright © Xist Publishing 2021
Illustration Copyright © Jenna Johnston 2021

Published in the United States
by Xist Publishing
www.xistpublishing.com
24200 Southwest Freeway
Suite 402- 290
Rosenberg, TX 77471

Hardcover ISBN: 978-1-5324-3176-0
Paperback ISBN: 978-1-5324-3175-3
eISBN: 978-1-5324-3174-6

Printed in the USA

KNOCK KNOCK, UNICORN WHO?
ILLUSTRATED UNICORN & MERMAID JOKES

Stephanie Rodriguez

Jenna Johnston

Knock knock.

Who's there?

You.

You, who?

Unicorn, that's who!

What does a mermaid use to call someone?

A shell phone.

Why did the unicorn cross the road?

It wanted to prove it wasn't chicken.

What is the most mythical vegetable?

The unicorn.

What is the difference between a carrot and a unicorn?

The first is a bunny feast,
the other is a funny beast.

Where does a mermaid keep her money?

In a riverbank.

What do you call a unicorn with no horn?

A horse.

How do unicorns get to the park?

On a unicycle.

Why did the mermaid ride the seahorse?

To play water polo!

How can you tell if a unicorn has a bad attitude?

She only says neigh.

Do they have unicorns at the zoo?

Yes – they're just big, grey and called rhinos.

Why do mermaids live in saltwater?

Because pepper makes them sneeze.

Why won't oysters lend money to mermaids?

Because they're shellfish.

What do unicorns call their dad?

Pop corn.

Knock knock.

Who's there?

Waldo.

Waldo who?

Waldo we need to go see a unicorn?

What did the sea say to the mermaid?

Nothing. It just waved.

What's a unicorn's favorite race?

A mare-athon!

What's a unicorn's favorite kind of story?

A fairy tale.

What do unicorns hang on Christmas trees?

Horn-aments.

What kind of bow can't be tied?

A rainbow.

Where does a mermaid sleep?

On a waterbed.

What do you call it when a unicorn wakes up for a midnight snack?

Star grazing.

What do unicorns and mermaids have in common?

The narwhal is their cousin.

Check out the other Illustrated Joke Books from Xist Publishing:

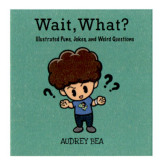
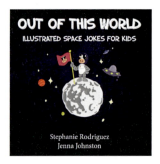
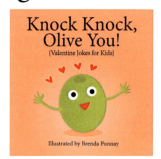

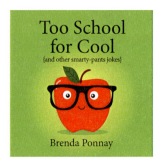
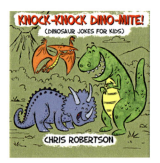
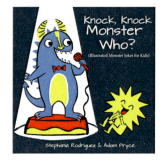
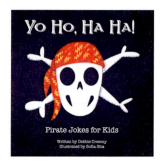

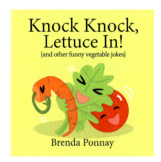
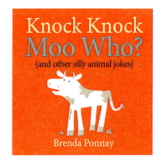
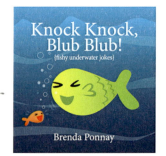
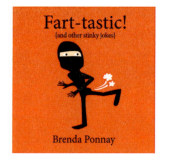

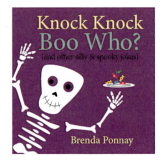
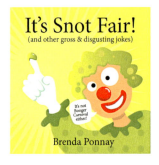
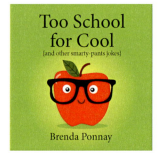